Terry Lovelette

IN PRAISE OF Eagle Mountain

Chapin Keith Publishing
Daleville, VA. 24083
www.chapinkeith.com

Publisher's Cataloging-in-Publication Data

Names: Lovelette, Terry - author.
Title: In Praise of Eagle Mountain / Terry Lovelette.

Identifiers: LCCN: 2025900546 | ISBN 979-8-9919038-3-7 (paperback) |
ISBN 979-8-9919038-4-4 (eBook).

Subjects: BISAC: POETRY / American / General.

Cover and book design by Asya Blue Design.

Cover photo by Terry Lovelette.

First Edition

CONTENTS

INTRODUCTION

We all travel the Milky Way together. Sometimes it's a rather strange journey. Chasing life in a fight to be right. Drenched by a shower of drama, chaos, and confusion. It can be hard to keep your heart light and simple in the midst of this crowd of madmen.

Instead of the wind among the spruce-tops and the rhythmic flow of the waterfalls, your ears get filled with the oaths and groans of a shallow world trying to find meaning within the self-induced churn. The crisp air of the mountains whispers a different tune.

While I typically take the advice of mystical wisdom and "wear the world like a loose garment," every once in a while, I just need to break away from the madness. To go into wild places where you have to depend on your intuition, on Nature's way, on a deeper sense of belonging. To find a place of quiet for a few hours, a day, a week, or a month.

We make a lot of noise in the rush of society. It's still possible to stay present in the middle of the rush, but I find that presence much more impactful in the splendor of nature. After all, it is our garden home and a place to connect with a power which is much greater than myself.

Philosophies abound and I appreciate that each person gets to choose their own path through life. In the adjoining poetry and prose, I'm offering perspectives gained from nature and from times when I have stepped away from the banter for a while. Whether on a wooded path, at a lake, or from going for a walk among the mountain tops, poetic thoughts flow. Then those musings resonate within and blossom in quiet locations, like Eagle Mountain. For me, they sing a music of praise, hope, and optimism that rests well on my ears. My hope is that you find some optimism and enjoyment in these musings too. May you find joy and inspiration as you read through *In Praise of Eagle Mountain*.

> *"No pessimist ever discovered the secret of the stars, or sailed an uncharted land, or opened a new doorway for the human spirit."*
> —Helen Keller

If Only for a Little While

Warm summer nights
Put to bed

The slow creep of autumn
Invites us in

In a rhythm of the season
Senses heighten

Accepting the invitation ahead
Recognition of shifting energies

Cradled in contemplative stillness
The artist works

Small patches of brilliance
Laid about

Brushstrokes of color
Highlight the earth

Beckoning our attention
Arranging the elements

The spiced smell of flora
Sprinkles the air

The scent of the forest
A time of terminal decay

In one vast miracle
Nature itself transcends

Bringing an expressive awe
Touching our deepest existential longing

Spreading creative tendrils
It paints in a poetic form of art

An antidote to forgetting our limitations
Opportunities to be present

Enough, at least, to live these moments
If only, for a little while…

AN INTERCONNECTED SPIRIT

"Be yourself; no base imitator of another, but your best self. There is something which you can do better than another. Listen to the inward voice and bravely obey that. Do the things at which you are great, not what you were never made for."
—Ralph Waldo Emerson -
Self-Reliance and Other Essays, 1803-82.

I don't know if I'm great at anything. But I do know that I am the best version of myself with regular time in nature. That's why I like to walk in wild places. I find a soul nourishment here and I come to my senses in ways that I haven't found possible in the churn of society. So, as Emerson suggests, I'm just being who I am. Thus, I come to the woods to get reacquainted with myself and the world around me.

In a manner that I don't fully understand, my mind quiets and I find the silent one inside. In that place of Grace, I hear the whispers from the earth. Wisdom lessons, that stretch beyond measurable time, form deep connections. There, I allow the light to fill me. In a subtle, unassuming way, it does. Beauty surfaces from a holy place and it's filled with an interconnected spirit. One that courses through all of creation. Unobstructed, like a fresh mountain stream. Within it, gratitude flows and appreciation for my place in the world surfaces with reminders of how to proceed. Each day and one day at a time...

In this Short Day

Be an example of kindness
Walk with a heart of compassion
Endure the moments with patience
Broaden your mind with understanding
Embrace the strength of tolerance
Sow mutual respect
Be open to the warmth of grace
Shine your light on dark places
Spread hope to all you greet
This is your one day
Live it well

The Hushed Embrace

In the hushed embrace of the season
Autumn awakes with a symphony of color
Moored in a cosmic rhythm of deep time
Yet it comes with a palpable immediacy

A whispered promise of serenity
Floats steady in the warm October air
Suspended in silence
Soaked by the chill of the night

Nature herself unveils the secrets
Displaying her most cherished palette
The world is reborn in shades of wonder
Each falling leaf an eternal dance
The mountain water flows
A soothing sound
Ripe fruit drops with a wistful thud
An abundant harvest offered

In the scent-scape of fall
The heart finds solace
It's important to go there
To be present
To see the falling of a leaf
To hear the rhythmic cadence of a stream
To watch a bird in flight

To witness your own thoughts
  scattered as they are
  chase each other
  through the forest of your mind

If you take the time
To engage your senses
Magical moments occur
Extraordinary riches are discovered

The childlike bickering
Of a restless world
Drifts away
Blown in the wind
Dispersed to their rightful place
Into the bottomless pit of oblivion

Then it comes
A peaceful presence
One not corrupted
Not aligned with any human agency

Tranquil and eternal
Beyond the veil of destruction
It's no longer a bother
In its place an Unseen Spirit

The lower vibrations of dualistic thoughts
Full of fear and arrogance
Become vulnerable and exposed

Absorbed by the plurality of Grace
We opt out of judgment
And ease into acceptance

Unnecessary irritations melt away
And the answers rest in love
...Always love

Our Gift from the Mountains

Embraced by the trail
we make our ascent
rhythmically climbing
determined intent
rocks and roots
dictate our pace
reminding us always
there's no need to race

With hearts beating fast
lungs gasping for air
we work every muscle
with little to spare
sweat soaks our backs
effort put forth
methodically moving
to make our way north

Together we walk
a tunnel of green
admiring beauty
of all that is seen
a peak of a mountain
magnificent views
carpets of moss
emerald hues
mushroom gardens

perfected with grace
alpine scent
a majestic place

treasure the moments
the two of us share
serenity comes
warmly in prayer
gifts freely given
from God above
examples of heaven
souls fill with love

HOPE REMAINS

L iving a life with spiritual beliefs means that sometimes you just have to hang on. Storms of uncertainty will continually blow in. At times delivered by a hurricane or through the cruel insensitivities of other human beings. Especially forceful when the obtuse go to battle backed by the power of their own fear and self-centered greed. Then, obscene actions (like war) are justified and enforced from a bully pulpit.

We all suffer in the wake of the relentless attacks. As Steinbeck said: "...it's not that evil ever wins, it's that it never goes away."

The divine essence lives within all of creation. In the words of Jewish philosopher, Martin Buber: "Where is the dwelling of God? God dwells wherever man lets him." When I let him dwell in me, I see his work in everything, even in those who deny his existence or dice up the divine with a Ginsu knife to satisfy their own self-centered needs.

As messy as we humans make it sometimes, keep the faith, hope remains when we remain hopeful. I offer some thoughts to consider in the following poem. (Maybe then we can see the truth.)

Out of the crucible which we come
Brings a sense of validation
Background, race, gender, politics, religion
Or not...

In our tribe
A perception of self is formed
Though fragile and uncertain
We settle and seek to belong

Beliefs build a foundation
A construct of acceptance develops
It steeps in a moldering mass
Ignorance stokes the decay
Simplistic solutions follow
The complexities of the world
Dismantled with a screwdriver

Society stays busy pointing fingers
An action that fuels an impulsive rush
Long-standing battle lines drawn
They define the dualism
Convinced of our identity we attack
The Ego is well fed and ready for battle

Truth becomes flexible
Twisted to fit the narrative
Morphed to manage an identity
A perception of morality injected
Self-righteous in its ways
It becomes an addictive drug

What is this notion of identity
Religious, ethnic, political, racial, national, or other
It has been one of the fundamental questions of our
    humanity
Jesus, Buddha, The Tao, The Shamans, The Stoics,
    and The Mystics
They all had much to say
But their words lay idle in a shackled mind

In the cosmic life
Our humanity is young
It is barely starting to discover its place
As we seek to uncover who we are
In the vast corridors of the universe, that we find
    ourselves in
May we wake up and realize what we share

While we continue to fight our differences
In a ritual form of power and control
A segmentation of self-centered values gets justified
Cannibalizing each other's humanity to the bitter end
Stoking the flames of hatred, evil, and destruction
Denying any responsibility
In a stubborn refusal of personal accountability
Minds rot in this toxic soup
The soul of our existence suffers

In our era of life
It takes strength to be better
To rise above the momentum of divisiveness

To be able to witness the great spectacle unfolding all
    around us
To develop the ability to become more honest with your
    own part in it
Then, to drill down to find a deeper truth
To recognize and accept one's own ignorance

Maybe there we can see the path forward
Maybe then we can read the words of wisdom clearly
    pointing the way
Maybe then we can cease our fight to be right
Maybe then we can accept ourselves as we are
Maybe then we can "love our neighbor as ourselves"
Maybe then we can find "the peace that surpasses all
    understanding"
Maybe then, we can see the truth, maybe then...

A Simple Man

A simple man
slanted views
opinions fly in vain

A simple man
firm lines drawn
a mindset held in chains

A simple man
raging thoughts
others are your bane

A simple man
soaring fears
such static in your brain

A simple man
the cause is lost
you see your plight inane

A simple man
once hardened soul
from anger you refrain

A simple man
awakened thoughts
your mission more humane

A simple man
A softer stance
grace will ease your pain

When the World Seems Troubled

When the world seems troubled
It comes at you hard
Remember to look upward
Not downward at yourself
Resist the temptation to lash out
To point the finger of blame
Look away from unpleasant surroundings
Be kind with dour dispositions
From the imperfections
In yourself and those around you
In that unrest
There is a place of calmness
Within impatience
A quiet pause
In limitations
A glimpse of perfection
Looking toward Grace
Sows' seeds of compassion
Fertilize them with radical empathy
This action enables your spirit to grow
Beauty will present itself
You will see something in it
Inspiration will brighten the gloom
Appreciation follows

As you grow your spiritual life
You will be enabled
You will do many things that seemed hard before
You will climb mountains
And those mountains will soothe your soul

The Eve of Winter Solstice

On the eve of winter solstice
Comes the slow creep of darkness
The earth tilts away from the sun
It creates the shortest days

There are secrets in the gray clouds
Revelations of thought in the cold winds
Decision points of action
Welcome them in

The soul of winter
An ancient inner journey
Ask yourself
What memory do I write

When the sun walks low on the horizon
Do I let the rays bring hope
Even when light is fleeting
Do I look for moments of joy

What will my next chapter be
Hidden deep within
On the long path of life
Are the reminders that brought us here

Drawn from the solitude
Whispers of inspiration
Reflections from the winter soul
Courageously persistent

When light and dark dance closely
Opportunity seeks us
From the deep well of time
An infinity of potential

Rest well this day
Embrace the Grace
The artwork of creation
On full display

Visions for the eyes
Wonders for the mind
Comfort for the heart
Soothing for the soul

A SNOWFALL IN THE WOODS

There's something magical about a snowfall in the woods. When you venture away from busy places, it brings a hush to the day. If you quiet yourself enough, you can hear the falling flakes.

Miraculous little works of art, these beautiful hexagonal shapes start as a tiny grain of dust. Little particles of cosmic clutter float along until a chance meeting with water vapor occurs. In the cold environment of the upper atmosphere the dust and water merge and freeze. In this frozen state the flake starts to grow in its supersaturated birthplace. One at a time, water molecules collect upon the developing flake. As they fall through the atmosphere, snowflakes grow in size as molecular droplets of water come together. Forming and reforming their way into ice crystals that most often have a hexagonal symmetry. Yet, as far as we know, each flake forms into its own unique shape.

In numbers that I don't know how to comprehend it happens. Through the formation of 10 quintillion (one quintillion is a billion billion) water molecules one unique snowflake is created. Although these microscopic creations are clear ice, the human eye perceives them as white through the reflective nature of the spectrum of light. Sometimes, you can see them sparkle and flash various colors as light passes through the collection of flakes. When the conditions are just right, it's as if you've walked into a kaleidoscope. Although an experience that is very rare, it's one that will leave you in complete awe!

We live in a beautiful place!

In Nature

In nature
If you quiet yourself
One can hear the silence
Feel the hum of the earth
Witness the rhythm of her breath
Sense the vibration of life
Being present enough to witness
The spectacular display is a gift
With little fanfare
It's revealed
Pause in appreciation
Embrace the ongoing display
Artistry unfolding in front of you
It's available everywhere
In everything
And all the time
We live in a beautiful place

The Winnowing on the Mountain

The clouded sky hung low
Gently above the mountain
Casting a soft hue
Amidst the landscape
Snow covered trees
Wrapped in a dreamlike blanket
Haunting expressions
Alien life forms appear
Each shape peaking from the forest
A quiet comfort nestled in the nooks
The prevailing winds
Winnowed the forest down
Creating the essence of the moment
In the grey-white boughs
From the soft eggshell color of the sky
A mystical presence greets the day
In the chill of the air
It casts a welcoming aura
Through the dim light
A subtle glow
The spirit of appreciation beckons
Touching the soul with a healthful splendor

Think on These Things in the Wonder of Life

We can be filled with wonder
By the halo of the sun
The faces of the frosted trees
The swiftly tilting planet
A stark mountain ridge
A genuine act of kindness

What amazes and inspires you today?
Is your spirit open to wonder
Are your eyes cast on beauty
Do you walk with love in your heart
Do you delight
   in this wonderful
   amazing
   unrepeatable
   moment of life

Pause throughout this day
Just be
Notice the wonder
Held softly in the simple things
   the beauty
   of the ordinary
   all around you

We get to choose our attitude
When we cultivate gratitude
We find a healthful joy

It spreads tendrils of happiness
It welcomes in companion thoughts
   optimism
   compassion
   respect
   acceptance
   generosity of spirit

Dark choices exist too
They empty the soul of life
Choose wisely

I trekked upon a mountain today
The clouds drained away
And the people too
We were alone the mountain and me
For a good long while we sat
I listened to the mountain's thoughts
Then with a wisp of wind
It sent me on my way
Today was a good day with the mountain

THE RIM OF THE GRAND CANYON

I suppose it happens, but I can't imagine anyone standing on the rim of the Grand Canyon and not being in complete awe. There is a reverence here that runs as deep as the river gorge. If you take but a minute, a deep humility resonates. Then, the eye of the soul opens, you become right-sized, and you see the magnificence of this amazing place in a meaningful way. Within that transition comes a hidden wholeness that embraces everything. It offers a warm awareness, leaves a lasting impression, and brings on a subtle joy. I simply call it Grace. It's a breeding ground, if you will, for a healthful gratitude. I'm fortunate enough today to appreciate this gift of life. Prayers of thanks are the only response that makes sense to me. We live in a beautiful place!

Reflections from Sedona . . .

In the grand expanse of the high desert
an ancient landscape unfolds
it tells a story of days gone by
times when life was different
geological history here unfolded slowly over a span of
500 million years or more
ocean bottoms
coastal plains
the thunderous roar of dinosaurs
uplifts
down faulting
volcanic activity
all slowly etched away by weather and time
humans arrived just 4000 years ago
probably they too sat in wonder over the beauty in front
of their eyes
most likely their sense of time and scale was much dif-
ferent than mine
that's probably a good thing
I enjoy thinking about how it all unfolded in the places
that we visit
sometimes though I ponder the plight of humanity as
well when I sit in these quiet locations
there we are chasing agendas
all wrapped up in ourselves
pissed off and angry at something or someone else
who's pissed off and angry
what a sad waste of time
but at the same time I can identify with the chase

I lived in it for quite a while
it's enjoyable to look at it through the rear-view mirror
now
like the buttes and mesas I'm a bit weathered
age and time will do that
yet I'm still here pressing on
thankful for the journey and the knowledge that above
my head in the great beyond there are over 100 billion
galaxies
each containing over 100 billion stars
all of this makes me feel small
but at the same time just right
like you I am here
somewhere amidst the insignificance of our collective
little place in time comes a purpose
one that is steeped in a perennial philosophy and
spreads throughout humanity in an interconnected
web of hidden wholeness
what anyone else chooses to call their philosophy mat-
ters little to me
instead I simply try to get out of the way and let mine
settle
in the process I find a deeper truth
with that truth comes an appreciation for life and grat-
itude for the universal Grace that holds it all together
from this eternal wellspring flows the reciprocity of love
a spirit that is holy
I remain hopeful that one day each one of us little bugs
will be touched by that Grace too
within it one can find their inner peace
and to me, that's where the hidden wholeness resides...

THE PROMISE OF SOLITUDE

Something pulled me toward Laraway Mountain today. Maybe it was the promise of solitude or perhaps the desire to visit a beautiful place that's most expressive in the winter. Whatever spurred me on I'm thankful for. Sometimes this location is quite majestic. The ice and light just simply need to be experienced in real time to best absorb the wonder. I'm always awestruck by natures artwork and with the creation of the varied ice formations. It leaves me humbled. Once again, I return home with a healthy reverence.

"It is the life of the crystal, the architect of the flake, the fire of the frost, the soul of the sunbeam. This crisp winter air is full of it."
—John Burroughs

AN ODE TO EVERETT RUESS

He tried to get over his deep mental obsession. But not even a 12-step program could help. Yes, the man had an incurable addiction. His mind often pulled him to places that he'd never been. A constant yearning tugged within. His boots needed to be put on the ground in wild places. Knowing that he could be eaten by a grizzly and become reincarnated as bear shit only made him dream more. The possibilities were endless and he was a hopeless case.

Wild Places

As you need air and water to live
I need wild places
Some don't understand the need
But Everett Ruess knew
Like him, I have not tired of the wilderness
…Alone, I shoulder the sky
Wind
rain
snow

ice
Raw but pure
Sunshine
a warm breeze
the desert sand
Welcomed friends
A gentle swaying of the trees
the whispers from the leaves
Music to my tired soul
Roots tangled into the cliff face
Reminders of inner strength
Seek
explore
roam the hidden places
Memories sanctified
...When we go, we leave no trace
...When we live, we find our place

Ulysses Burns Within Me

A beckoning wind blows my way
The call of travel to a distant land

For you see
Ulysses burns within me

I yearn to walk in unknown places
Ne'er a mission to escape life

But a journey to its core
Riches of the earth

Soothe like drops of rain
Restorative powers

Immersed
In the endless beauty of nature

Shackles of bondage
Shed their grip

Mountains embrace
Majestic glory

Wild places
Serve to tame the restless mind

Freedom cleanses my soul
And the Grace of Divine Love burns anew

The Lookout

Walk to a lookout
Sit for a spell
Let thoughts settle
All is well
Take in the views
From the world below
Listen intently
The trees gently sough
Thermals catch
The Corvids wing
Delightful dance
Here they are king
Warmth of the sun
Upon my face
Tranquil moments
Move at their pace
Restorative energy
Flows into my pores
Societal angst
A waning allure

TERRY LOVELETTE

The Spirit of Truth

The spirit of truth
brings an appeal
A noble objective
Of all that is real

Brought to the day
As a mission of faith
Or maybe a ploy
Meant to bring scathe

Man and his mission
Not always pure
Deceit clouded messages
A seductive lure

Speaking words
For earthly gain
Bending the truth
Inflicting pain

Somewhere a ledger
Quite likely is kept
An ultimate fate
Is sure to be met

Thoughts can get murky
Hope might seem lost
Yet keep yourself honest
It comes at no cost

The Daily News

Discord flows
From the daily news
Perpetual madness
With no excuse

Dramatic stories
Come with great flair
The masses tune in
To the morning despair

Coffee warm
For a rested soul
Wake up slowly
To the earthly toil

Conditioned to listen
To spoon fed tracks
Apocalyptic themes
Seep through the cracks

Beautiful people
Aesthetic appeal
Spinning the slant
Of another sad reel

Casual effect
Or lessons by rote
Reactions follow
Societies dope

Addicted to drama
We wax in discord
Tension mounts
Misery scored

Tune in at 11
The latest just in
Brainwash to continue
Never an end

A WALK...

Some time ago I took a walk. Innocuous as it was, I trudged along. Nobody knew about my walk, I just went. In a dream like state I meandered, the clamor of society abated. No gossip, drama, whining, and no pissing and moaning about all the things that most of us piss and moan about.

So, I walked. As I walked, I awoke. When I awoke, I saw things. Bugs, bees, flowers, trees, rivers, streams, lakes and tarns. I saw the land rise into hills and saw the hills roll into mountains.

So, I walked. As I walked, I embraced. When I embraced, I felt things. The rhythm of the bugs and the buzz of the bees. The beauty of the flowers and the sway of the trees. The flow of the river and the babble of the stream. The motion of the lake and the tranquility of the tarn. The warmth of the hills and the starkness of the mountains.

So, I walked. As I walked, I listened. When I listened, I heard things. Bugs munching on leaves and bees busy collecting nectar. Rivers making their way and streams working to catch up. Lakes washing against their shore and the endless ripples of the mountain tarn. The crunch under my feet as I passed from hill to mountain.

So, I walked. As I walked, I lived. When I lived, I found gratitude. Grateful for the gift of sight to see things more clearly. Grateful for the gift of awareness that comes from an awakening. Grateful for the gift of embracing the moments and for being present. Grateful for the gift of hearing so that I can be open to the sounds of the earth. Grateful for the gift of life so that I can continue to love.

So, I walked...

The Coming of Spring

Warmth in the morning
Of a springtime thaw
Nature at work
Irrepressible laws

Spirits lifted
Energy restored
Hope fills my heart
Thanks to the lord

Gratitude reached
I lay down to sleep
Visions of flowers
Dreams to keep

Awake in the morning
I climb out of bed
Rubbing my eyes
Scratching my head

What happened outside
As my dreams made their way
A blanket of snow
Greeting my day

My mood takes a hit
Mouth agape
Where is spring
No more can I take

Longing for sunshine
I cry at the sight
Why oh why
Must we endure such a plight

Sunshine I need
Not a blanket of white
Help ease my pain
Take away winters bite

Alas comes the message
From a heavenly glow
Change takes time
In the seasonal flow

Embrace this day
And the moments they bring
Patience my son
Soon you'll see spring

A High Desert Mesa

On a high desert mesa, the horizon is distant
As the sun sinks low it takes on a warming glow
Molecular magic bends the fading light through the
   atmosphere
Sunlight scatters and cast a prismatic affect

Distant mountains absorb the tones
Clouds reflect a looming presence
Eternities become moments as images form
Shapes illuminate a majestic appeal

Reverent thoughts flood the brain
I struggle to comprehend
Colors change in the blink of an eye
A motion picture of divine awe

There are no walls here
Humanities clamor is muted
Societies discontent abated
Fearful souls left behind

No agenda to achieve or point to be made
The drive to be right not relevant
Equanimous moments have that result
Nature always effects a cure

If we seek hell on earth then we cannot know heaven
If heaven is our pursuit, then there is no hell
For those who seek find
To those who knock, the door is always opened

Listen to the Natural World

I love days like today
You just follow the urging
It kicks in the will to move

The body set in motion
On a trail of mud and snow
In the quiet of the woods

A silent solitude settles in
With the rhythm of the walk
The mind releases clutter

Listening ears are opened
Framing observant eyes
The fragrant forest
An olfactory delight

It's necessary
To step away
To spend time with nature
To ease the busy world

Wilderness waits
Just around the corner
Not far from the bustling pace

Stand near the water's edge
The still lake beckons
A peaceful calm

Hills of trees
Geese in rest
Cloud dotted skies
Reflections of serenity

The natural world abounds
Always speaking to us
Waiting for listening ears
Watchful eyes
Receptive minds
Appreciative hearts

Wherever you are
Take the moment
Listen to the natural world
Hear it with your soul
Only then
Can you know what it says

The Flow of Grace

The day begins in a gentle way
Fresh snow on the ground
Sun peeking through the trees

Look out the window
A peaceful scene awaits
Breath in the tenderness

Shared freely
By the morning light
Bouncing softly through the trees

Dark silhouettes
In reflective dance
The forest shines

Branches take in color
Sparkling flakes
A peaceful presence

Held in silence
Drifts of white
On moss covered rocks

The day opens wide
From this tranquil place
A warm softness

It's full of life
Slow the pace
Rest in serenity

Embrace the flow of Grace

What is Poetry

In a world full of wonder
Learn things anew
It will never fail you
Always true

A walk in the forest
Springtime fresh
Sunshine and shadows
Yugen bliss

Drop the misery
Of cruel fearful men
Swindlers and scoundrels
Selfish within

Instead reap the joy
From the wisdom of yore
Seek courage to journey
Our heartstrings implore

Flowers break through
A long winters rest
Colorful glory
Serenity's best

Ghost-like visions
Float through the trees
White flags flashing
Darting with ease

Never exhausted
This beauty of place
Natures abundance
The essence of Grace

A GRATEFUL PERSPECTIVE

*"...a grateful perspective brings happiness and
abundance into a person's life."*
—Jones from The Noticer

I'm a writer and a poet. That doesn't make me better than
anyone else. It doesn't make me worse than anyone else
either. It simply makes me who I am. So, I write. Sometimes,
when the spirit moves me, I openly share what I write. It's a
pathway for me that allows the expression of inner thoughts.
Others have their own way of expressing themselves. I do my
level best to be respectful and listen to others with ears of under-
standing, not judgement. I'm never perfect with this approach.
Yet by listening to understand I have a better chance of silencing
the ego and hearing with the soul. When I listen to respond, the
ego becomes fully engaged, I stop understanding and the urge to
interrupt becomes overwhelming. A sure sign for me that I need
to refocus and not say anything. Then re-engage with an under-
standing heart. For me a practice of progress, not perfection.

Recently, the universe has been showing me what it feels like
to be attacked. Disrespectful messages have come my way. This

type of feedback has been happening to writers for eons. It's not unique to me and it comes with the territory. I accept it for what it is. After all, I accept the favorable feedback. I would be in a place of great angst if I didn't allow others to have a voice and shine their light, however they choose to do it. Frankly, rude interruptions from another are a great gift. Those moments provide an opportunity to make a choice. Pick up a stick and fight back or show some compassion and kindness? An easy decision to make from the outside looking in. Not as easy when you are the one taking the brunt of someone's egocentric impulses. In those situations, it's difficult to keep your cool and remain sane. When I'm able to maintain some element of composure in those moments, it's the result of countless quiet hours of prayer. Somehow God's Grace ushers in a response and it's always better than mine. I'm beyond grateful to know this truth today.

Here is the poem that has stirred a few folks up.

I must be the one who's crazy...

I've been listening a lot lately
Trying to take it in

Watching folks talk at each other
Words fill the air
They drift with the breeze
Would it help if I said something
You know, be a voice of reason
Maybe a suggestion
To calm down a bit
Try a little respect

I do that
My words drift away too
In the big picture
Nobody knows me
Fewer people care
That's okay
It's none of my business anyway
I'm glad that I know this truth
For that
I say thank you
A simple prayer
The choice of Love
Full of Grace
Like Emerson
"Glad to the brink of fear"
Peaceful and serene

What's the other choice?

Feed the rage
Sit in silence and brood
Ruminate in the misery
Sometimes it feels good
To feel bad
Self-pity
Fear
The Ego's cold embrace
A suffocating little monster
It will swallow you whole
Listen to the noise
Shake your head at the chaos

Linger in distractions
Latch on to the nonsense
The drama of things
It'll always keep you busy
Lock you up even
In your own little prison
Wallowing in thought
You become a toxic brew
It's trendy to rant
Spew your anger
Somebody will pat your back
A ritual form of validation
It will justify your misery
For a minute

Every now and again
I sit there

Wondering about it all
Angry rants
Random violence
Weapons of mass destruction
It once seemed far away
In distant corners of the world
Fearful people in anguish
Hellbent on destruction
It isn't far away anymore
Mainstream madness
Ideological rigidity
Normalized insanity
The fight to be right

Thuggery has evolved
Now it comes from everywhere
Presidents and Politicians
Dictators and Dignitaries
Doctors and Lawyers
Preachers and Teachers
Farmers and Factory workers
Rotarians and Librarians
Burly guys with beards
Bleached blond ladies with Jesus tattoos
Common folks too
Some of them with PHD's
Sadly
From 6-year-olds
With a gun
Just pick a side and abide
Grab a stick
Beat the person next to you
It's what we do now

None of it makes sense to me
I must be the one who's crazy

THE NORTHERN LIGHTS

I't's wonderful to see so many beautiful pictures of the northern lights display this morning. Impactful beauty exists in nature everywhere and all the time. Once you give yourself permission to absorb the immensity of it all, you never look at life the same way again. Quite literally, this beauty is a wakeup call to anyone who is ready and willing to receive the message to slow down the pace and appreciate life to the fullest.

Society likes to keep us on the run. Consequently, we move too fast, too restlessly, too feverishly. So much so that we forget to pay attention to what's happening in the here and now. We miss life as it unfolds right before our very eyes because our vision is fixated on the chase. After all, it's exciting. Drama, chaos, and confusion draw us in and keep us busy. Slow it down and taste the one small moment. No exotic travel is required to see the beauty of creation. It's everywhere and all the time. Once you give yourself permission to see it, a warm embrace follows, and you are welcomed into a place of incomprehensible joy. Then, you see beauty like you never did before.

Although I try, I find it difficult to come up with the words to describe that beauty. It's so compelling that language just doesn't do it justice. Instead, it's more of an experience that is really spiritual at a personal level. Somehow one can feel big and small, significant and insignificant, fearful and fearless, all at the same time. Nature just finds a way into you and it changes your earthly perceptions in an extremely positive manner. As it is, one leaves better for these experiences and they send you off with a lasting fortitude.

Sitting in the middle of magnificence displays in nature offer moments that can be carried with you. The beauty of it is, you can't plan it. By being outside and into nature, these experiences simply happen. Ephemeral moments where light, landscape, and emotion collide in a spectrum of magic and beauty. When "in the moment" I'm not always aware that it's occurring. Only afterwards can I fully appreciate the complete euphoria and splendor. Wonderful memories that can never be taken away. We live in a beautiful place!

THE DESIRE TO WALK

lthough my pace is slowing down, I haven't lost my desire to walk. Being out in the mountains, or in a quiet forest, are locations that help me find meaning. Springtime brings fresh renewal. The ground is fully nourished from the winter snowmelt. Flowers and leafy vegetation sprout. They bring a fragrance to the day and create poetic imagery that can transfer you to a different world. Quite often I find that when I unplug my busy brain, and plug in to the presence of nature, moments of clarity work their way.

Not that I have any great epiphanies or make life changing discoveries that no one else has ever thought of. Yet it's safe to say that I often walk myself into my best thoughts. At times these thoughts flow through me and offer perspectives that I might not have considered. Facing myself and my own stubborn way of thinking seems to come easier when I'm making my way along a trail. Reason enough for me to make sure that I spend some quality time by myself. After all, I need to breathe, and I need to be. Why not do some of that in the mountains? Opting for silence and solitude sets the conditions right for my own well-being.

That doesn't make me antisocial or mean that I reject the rest of the world. It just means that I'm doing my best to take care of myself in a way that helps me engage more seamlessly into the world around me.

It also helps me understand that I am but a very small part of a much greater whole. This brings about an awareness of my surroundings. Like, who's chewing on the trail signs? Maybe someone's dog or maybe a restless bear? So, my focus gets heightened. That focus tunes me in to the sounds of the woods and it enables me to see deeper into the forest. Perhaps I found the guy who's chewing on the sign, or maybe like me, he doesn't want to be bothered while he's enjoying his walk. Either way, we left each other alone and got on with the day. We live in a beautiful place!

LIMITLESS INSPIRATION

I t's beautiful to be alone in the mountains. Especially on a day when the weather is a bit off. Folks seem to stay away, the trails are quiet, and the noise is down. What you're left with is untainted solitude. It's a place that I cherish and appreciate.

At 66, I don't get after it like I use to. But I still enjoy a good walk in the mountains. Seemingly, it's the place that offers me limitless inspiration. In some mysterious way Grace meets me there and moves me to places where I haven't been yet. How and why this works is beyond me. I just do my best to let things go and welcome in this radical acceptance.

It always comes with a childlike joy that raises my awareness. Simple things present themselves to me. They offer wonder and curiosity. In the creation that we coexist in, the spirit of reciprocity flourishes. With an unspeakable language, prayer is exchanged in the most natural manner. Silence.

I'm reminded time and again to not take myself too seriously. In fact, I'm reminded to not take any of it too seriously. It's a common practice for humanity to get bogged down in the gloom of life. Our current society isn't unique in that regard. Forever, our kind has lived in this tragic comedy. One that is steeped in the unrest of egocentric angst. Religious followers have names for this. I call it me and I call it you. Collectively we walk on the edge of the precipice. On the one side, the depths of fear and the other side the mountain of faith. Throughout it all, one is never truly alone. In the miraculous journey of life, a guiding force is centered within and always with us. When we listen to the guidance, we are reminded that there is nothing wrong with life as it is. It's the choices made that matter. It is in our power as human beings to say yes to life and to not destroy the spirit which illuminates each individual.

In the creative world of the spirit, the holy exists. In the stillness comes the idea to accept life on life's terms. That radical acceptance opens the gateway to inner peace and it enables a lasting serenity.

We live in a beautiful place!

MICRO-MOMENTS OF GRATITUDE

Thank you! Last night our neighbor sent us a text to look at the rainbow in our backyards to the east. At the same time, and to the west, there was a magnificent sunset. Like a warm embrace, you get to silently appreciate it. As the Fourth of July is upon us. Maybe take a moment or two and pause with appreciation, as it's nice to know that, once in a while, misery doesn't need any more company. Amidst the gloom of imperfection rests a quiet Grace. There, micro-moments of gratitude exist. Let them in. We live in a beautiful place!

It's Nice to Know

It's nice to know that once in awhile
Someone is thinking of you

It's nice to know that once in awhile
Kindness rules the day

It's nice to know that once in awhile
Silent scars have a lot to say

It's nice to know that once in awhile
These scars leave regrets

It's nice to know that once in awhile
Another soul will need to dump the angst

It's nice to know that once in awhile
You will be their receptacle

It's nice to know that once in awhile
Someone else has listened to you

It's nice to know that once in awhile
Reciprocity exists

It's nice to know that once in awhile
Empathy has no intellect

It's nice to know that once in awhile
Compassion requires no tongue

It's nice to know that once in awhile
The warrior soul has fought battles

It's nice to know that once in awhile
Damage was done and marks were left inside

It's nice to know that once in awhile
Each person holds a vessel of inner pain

It's nice to know that once in awhile
Touching that place is an awkward dance

It's nice to know that once in awhile
Sorrow brings a quiet shame

It's nice to know that once in awhile
Expression will come through blame

It's nice to know that once in awhile
Grace allows a sacred honor

It's nice to know that once in awhile
Love will truly shine

It's nice to know that once in awhile
Rainbows show bright in the backyard

It's nice to know that once in awhile
A beautiful sunset glows outside your front door

It's nice to know that once in awhile
You can slow down the chase of life

It's nice to know that once in awhile
Being okay is okay

It's nice to know that once in awhile
There is beauty in existence

It's nice to know that once in awhile
Your neighbor will remind you to look at it

It's nice to know that once in awhile
You get to appreciate a moment of silence

It's nice to know that once in awhile
You aren't alone

A MISTY MOUNTAIN TOP

I like a misty mountain top. There in the sweet solitude it all slows down. As the fog quietly rolls around you can hear the evaporating water droplets effervesce. The sun works through the dense blanket formed by the cool collection of dew drops from the night before. Gently warming the day and parting the vapor bath that weighs heavy in the air. Birdsong reverberates in the quietude of the morning. Somehow, the elements of the day work their way inside of you. Touching your heart and soothing your soul. Artfully, they slowly sculpt away and smooth all of the sharp edges chiseled by a restless world.

I recall a few words from a kindred spirit on what it means to be free. In the words of Gary Snyder: "Free means being, for one thing. It means being able to outgrow that knee-jerk reflection of what your human society around you wants you to think - and so 'free' means thinking for yourself and not accepting every piece of information or opinion heedlessly."

However mean and unruly life seems to be, meet it and live it. Running away or gearing up to fight yet another battle won't yield a peaceful result. Certainly, you'll find company in your misery but there you will be. Just another fault-finder who is pointing a finger and laying blame. For those folks, even paradise is not enough.

In a parallel space, far away from the impulsive allure, there is abundant beauty existing as God's creation and working its way in the precious moments of the day. Beauty, if you will, is everywhere and all the time. But you have to choose to live in the present in order to see it. Then, allow for the warm embrace in order to be it. Truly, if you do, you will be launched into a tranquil place and find your eternity in these micro-moments of life. It's possible to stitch the moments together and enable the whispers of the peaceful Presence help you become better, not bitter. For me, a reasonable approach.

I've discovered that the longer I live within this Presence, the more beautiful it all becomes. Even the angry rants of spiteful souls offer a healing message. If one chooses to ignore the beauty, then one will soon be without it. An impoverished darkness will ensue and one's vision becomes obscured. But when you choose to invest in the beauty of life, the fog will lift, and you will be enriched by an aura of serenity. Always there, just for you, may you find that too!

Walking in the Quietude

No one sees me
As I walk the wooded path
People pass by
Selfie stick in hand
Chattering thoughts
Talking at each other
Is anyone listening?

The deer in the bushes
Shakes it's head
Birds stop their song
Mouths agape
Quietly suspended
In disbelief

You can't hear the stream
When the busy brain roars
You can't see the forest
With selfies galore

It takes a minute
For the noise to disperse
The obtuse banality
Lingers in the air
Gentle breeze
Sweeps it away

I climb many mountains
Not to be seen
But to see the world
It's easy to feel like a holy man
While standing on a mountain top
That's not being free
It isn't about me

What belongs to you
In your very own life
Where the heights
Of your interior
Ridge lines exist
Is how you live

Words fill the air
Look at me moments
Shatter the way
Judgmental jargon
Clutters our thoughts
Throw a pithy quote
Or two
Sprinkle in
A ten word meme
Maybe a Bible verse
It feels so good
To be right

In the never-ending saga
The life history
  Of the human race

Unfolds
Full of torment
Sated by greed
The mammons EGO
Constant need

What lesson do you heed?

See yourself in the weeds
Wisdom lends a hand
Nudging you along
Toward the path of freedom
My way is one way home
Yours, another
Rest kindly here
    Help each other along

In good works
It's very simple
The "Golden Rule" applies
One can give without loving
But you can never love
Without giving
Small gestures
In the mundane world
    Matter most
Through compassion
    You bring Love

Then, you will know
    And

You will never be lonely again
A subtle joy will Grace your day
Unrest drifts away

In the tumultuous world
It doesn't matter
If you're seen
You will be okay
The way home
Will appear

It's the path
Of tranquil beauty
Walk in the quietude
It's waiting for you
    To follow...

YOUR FAVORITE PATH

"Pursue some path, however narrow and
crooked, in which you can walk with
love and reverence."
—Henry David Thoreau

Research finds that mindfulness increases positivity and decreases anxiety and negativity. Take time to improve your overall mood, physical well-being, and mental health by spending time walking or hiking your favorite path. I know that I learn a little bit more about myself every time that I do.

Make a choice to be

The mountains tell us we need silence
If we're to hear the speaking of our soul

The songbird tells us to hush
If we're to hear the gifted song

The ripples of the water tell us to keep quiet
If we're to hear the rhythm of the earth

The sturdy rock reminds us to harken the words of
the wise
If we're to hear the messages of wisdom

The rushing wind tells us to listen
If we're to hear the strength of the bending tree

The heavy clouds say persevere
If we're to hear the power of the distant thunder

The peeks of sun say heed the light
If we're to hear the persistence in the rays of hope

If we do we make a choice to be
Then, the world is right

Upon Awakening

Awakened in the morning
By the suns early glow
The crisp air chills
Mountains sough

Light of the day
Its warmth abounds
Darkness wanes
A new day crowned

Serene moments pass
Nature stirs
A deer munching grass
Dew drips from a fir

Aesthetic reflections
Shine from below
Equanimity reached
Tranquility grows

Surrender to the reverence
That nature brings
Open my ears
As the songbird sings

Life in abundance
Getting on with its duty
Each with a mission
Graced in beauty

Gratitude reached
A soul touched deep
Tears in my eyes
I gently weep

The worldly din
So far away
Divine is the present
I long to stay

Alas comes the message
From somewhere within
My place isn't here
The delusion ends

Belongings packed
The trail awaits
Time to move on
My stride hits its gait

Around each corner
Adventures anew
Inner resolve
I always make do

Embracing these moments
Enriches my life
The wilderness world
Eases my strife

GUIDING YOU HOME

"It is no small thing to speak your truth in a time of propaganda and misinformation. It is no small thing to seek the common good when humanity has broken down into warring tribes. It is no small thing to live in joy, not because one has arrived at the beloved community, but because one realizes the incredible importance of walking a noble though lightless path into a new and better day."

—Jim Rigby

Live Graciously

The sun sets orange
In the western sky
A loon call echoes
In the stillness
Serenity fills the soul
Quietude and wonder

In a high and holy place
Comes this force of life

The shape of meaning
The shape of memory
The shape of hope
The pathway of love

It revives the lowly spirit
Inspiring the heart of the contrite

Life is a challenge
In twisted times
Suffering can linger

Grasping the sides
Poking at the misery
Stories are created

Villains appear
Targets for displacement

Peppered in the back
With poisonous arrows
From an archer of vengeance

Behind the bow
Emptiness
Deep sorrow
Projections self defense
This method lends no cure

Witnessing your life
Through the lens of the soul
Brings along a truth
Profundity at the core
Even in the most difficult times
Find some space

Negative emotions settle
Slowly dropping
Into the distant horizon
Radical acceptance
Comfort and ease

In the tranquil place
A healing Grace hovers
While we stumble
Along the way
Take heart
Heed the calling

The divine light
Always present
In the actual life
A beacon to follow
With joy a solemn oath
Live graciously with faith
It will guide you home

TODAY IS A GOOD DAY

Each day, and one day at a time, I start my day by saying Thank You. Why? Because it's important for me to start my day with an awareness to cultivate the spirit of gratitude. With it comes an underlying joy, as well as an appreciation for life. I'm not boasting about this truth because it doesn't come from me.

Frankly, the more that I get out of the way, the better it gets. Letting go and letting God brings in a tranquil way. The mind becomes calmer, the heart holds more love, and peace rests in the soul. From that place of acceptance, I have a chance to focus on my own set of quirks and idiosyncrasies. The more effort that I apply to improving myself the more accepting I am of everyone else. I'm fortunate today to be able to realize these truths.

I get a chance each day to honor this Grace by doing my best to be of service to others and to live a purposeful life. Today is a good day to remember where it all comes from, Thank you.

"Cultivate the habit of being grateful for every good thing that comes to you, and to give thanks continuously. And because all things have contributed to your advancement, you should include all things in your gratitude." - Ralph Waldo Emerson.

What's not to be grateful for? I wish each of you the very best in your journey. Keep the faith!

THE SERENE FLOW OF LIFE

I woke up before the birds this morning, I listened to the crickets chirping away, it brought on a good mood.

Often, before the day begins and the first rays of sun shine some light, there is a peaceful quiet born from a silent night. Once in a while, there is a soft breeze that brings along the fresh scent of the earth and whiffs of morning flowers. Nearby, a rustle in the hedgerow reminds me that another world exists. One devoid of human drama, chaos, and confusion. It's a healthy place to spend time.

Once you experience the serene flow of life, you realize that it's about the simple choices. Really, if you allow yourself to go there, you will never find yourself wanting more than what's in front of you. Somehow an intuitive understanding of joy finds its way in and it ushers the din of society out. The trivial grandiosity of life goes along with it. Then there's nothing to fight. No fear to focus on and no ego to fuel the flames of a self-centered will.

There's just a tranquil way and a peaceful path to follow. Call it what you will, but I suggest that you move toward it and follow along, it makes all the difference.

A Home of Perennial Promise

It's quiet at the lake
Calm waters ripple
There's a peculiar stillness

Fish jump and splash
Birds chirp and flutter
Trochilidae's buzz
The great hum of life
Joyful and harmonious

Odd in our restless times
In a society teetering on madness
From a populace of zombies
Disillusioned and edgy
Manufacturing enemies
In a stream of angry rants

With a semiconscious walk
Seeking attainment
Following a path of breadcrumbs
Into the abyss of the status quo
Sated by the misery
Starving inside
Shrouded by darkness

An aura of melancholy
Settles like a fog
Obstructing the beauty

With a wisp of wind
A ray of light
Sun and air
Nature's medicine

There is lighthearted laughter
In the rising sun
She brings the Divine spirit
Let her have its way

Grace will soothe the heart
Refreshing your tired body
Curing your troubled mind
Nourishing the soul
Bask in the warm embrace

What is hidden in you
Will emerge
From the serene shadowed shelter
A tranquil authentic peace

May it spark your inner light
That springs a new appearance
One that forms revived perceptions
With new understandings
Enlightened pathways of thought

There are blessings along the way
Waiting to be discovered
Each one a gift for you
May you live in the sunshine

Let it burst from within
It will illuminate your vision
Enhance the spirit of reciprocity
Bring acceptance from a deeper well

May we all be energized
By the beauty
From this redeeming
Flow of life
A restful place
Full of kindness
An uplifting beacon of hope

A home of perennial promise

THE FLEETING DANCE OF LIFE

Thanks everyone for the birthday wishes! Your thoughtful messages are heartwarming! Starting year 66 in the most routine way. In the quiet of the morning and in the comfort of our place.

In the fleeting dance of life, a delicate balance of moments unfolds before us. Each one a birth of opportunity that comes with the gift of choice. As it goes, this day and the breath that it brings, will come and never return quite the same way again. Thus, it makes little sense to me to ignore the moments or to leave them for later. So why not take them as they come then greet them with an opened heart and outstretched arms? Life unfolds in the micro-moments. In the place where seeds of the future are planted in one's own garden of perception. Kindly nurture those seeds while fertilizing them with hope and inspiration. Tending to the inner landscape in this manner brings personal growth, purpose, and Grace. For me, a reasonable approach.

In the middle of it all, you realize that when you pursue your passion you become graced with wonder. Then, it all starts to reveal itself in a purposeful way within the intricate detail of nature. The dullness of the world melts away and you get to experience the multitude of wonder that exists within everything. Always there and available to anyone who chooses to see.

So much of our experience depends on how we look at things and what actions we choose to take. My experience is that the quality of my looking determines what I allow myself to see. All that I need to do is accept the invitations that are freely sent my way. When I do accept them, the mystery and beauty of nature illuminates the world. The stuff that's never talked about stirs inside into a healthy blend of inner peace. An interconnected love, if you will, that holds it all together. It's everywhere, all the time, we only need to choose to see it and allow ourselves to be it.

To all of you; be kind to each other and follow your passion. Therein lies a purpose that comes with a meaningful Grace. No matter what the circumstances are in life, keep moving forward, the best is yet to come. Much love and respect to you and yours!

FIND A QUIET PLACE

It's always enjoyable to go out for a walk. Nothing grandiose or spectacular. Just go to a quiet place where pine fresh forest scents help cleanse the mind. Where light creates poetic imagery that smoothly transforms you into another world. In a subtle way you discover a rate and pace to the day that's more wholesome and organic. Stumbling upon a deep meaning to life or having multiple epiphanies that no other soul has ever experienced is not the point. Living within the peaceful realm of solitude is reward enough. Somehow it all flows within, to that serene place where the origin of breath exists, and the essence of Grace brings its tranquil way. Of all the possible choices to make, going out for a walk seems like a reasonable thing to do.

TWISTED TIMES

T hese are twisted times. An air of melancholy hovers thick like the morning mist. At every turn, it seems, you listen to another person's lament. Moans of discontent echo from the hollows. Full of despair and pining for a mysterious hope. Follow this path to the depths of depression if you must. Let it wrap you up in a cloak of darkness. It will gladly welcome you in.

Yet, we can't lose heart. While it might seem that the world is wasting away, inwardly each one of us is being renewed day by day. Perennial wisdom points the way and offers trail blazes to follow.

Winter winds blow an arctic chill. In the mysterious pace of nature, we awake one morning to a silver silence. All around us there is quiet beauty. Artwork from a higher order paints the landscape with the colors of the season. I feel a little hope rise in the wonder of this place. Peaceful moments that are absent of conflict. A presence of Grace hangs steady in the shadows. Reminders of how perseverance can create a bridge that leads to a greater purpose and heals the ancient wounds from the deep well of compassion.

From this profound stillness comes a silent invitation to let go of the chaos that we carry. It's not there just for those who think like us, but for each person who crosses this path. The eyes of the Bard Owl reach into your soul and touch that special place. In that moment, you are reminded that peace does not come from the chase. Instead, it's something that you feel when you put down your club and stop fighting life.

When you do, the turbulence inside begins to settle. Then, from the wellspring of your inner resolve comes a calm mind, a loving heart, and a peaceful soul. Surprisingly, you discover that it was always there. All you needed to do was pause, look around, and let it find you.

In the spirit of the season, maybe it's a good time to remember a few important realities. Your neighbors' tears could be your own and their laughter could be yours. In this delicate dance of life, we are all bound together. As we work our way trying to make sense of our human condition, choices made in the micro-moments matter. Each life touches another in ripples that we seldom get to see. What messages are you sending out to the world? Important considerations to ponder. Because what you send out returns tenfold. Misery? Or God's Grace? Choose wisely. This day is your one chance at life. Live it well.

THE SLOW CREEP OF AUTUMN

The slow creep of autumn seeks its place. In the rhythm of time, it works in the background. Speaking nature's language, the gift of silence, poverty, solitude, joy, where everything is touched and turned into prayer. Sparked by shorter days and chilly nights. Heavy dew weighs the grass. The spiced scents of the season. Shifting pigments of color work, a subtle transition. If we allow ourselves enough humility a chance happening occurs. The cynical mind of our times gives way to a sacred independence. Then, we get to see things with a deeper appreciation. One that brings a new perspective and a lighter heart. Offer yourself this choice: It can keep you from dying before you're dead.

Who Brought You Here this Morning

Who brought you here this morning
As you warm the silent lake

I'm not sure that I'm ready for you now
Sleep lingers in my eyes

Yet your shine drifts at the water's edge
A daily glow of restorative light

I see an otter swim in the morning mist
A subtle ripple follows

The loon's call echoes in the air
Hauntingly beautiful it rests in the heart

An Osprey dives for its morning meal
Splashing a rhythm of orange tinted waves

In these quiet times one can regain a sense of discovery
An essence of your life's journey in the flow of the universe

When you allow your heart to see
Reverence unfolds around you

Moments of beauty braid into your days
Your mind becomes richer

It opens a pathway to the soul
Where light and grace elegantly shine

Lake Carmi can be the vessel of inner peace
If only one pauses and sees

Then this destination of wonder shines a gracious light
It brings a sense of meaning that ushers in rays of hope

MEMORIAL DAY THOUGHTS

I n an act of remembrance, many folks hold family gather-
ings on Memorial Day weekend. As ours concluded, I took
a moment to rest in gratitude. To think about a lifetime of
memories that Lake Carmi holds within its waters. For each of
us, a story that's unique. But also one rife with an interconnected
and mutual Grace. I wish all of you a great summer season and
may we all continue to embrace the beautiful place that we get
to live in. All the best!

Memories of the Lake

It's good to remember
To feel the way
One that can't be spoken
The eternal way

On the shore of the lake
It feels like the past is near
Visions of history
Come rippling in

Like the waves of time
They shimmer
Glistened by the sun
Warmth touches the soul

Happy visions follow
Difficult to hold
They stand on the rim
Too beautiful to swallow

When the sun drops low
The evening air turns blue
The Bard Owl
Calls to the rising moon

A golden hue
Settles in the water
It is then a reflective dance
Its strangeness becomes apparent

A million memories glisten
From a world invisible to me
On the cusp of present time
Voices echo

The unseen place beckons
A sound of perfection
Discernible in fragments
Voices from a universal Love

Amidst the bonfires and barbecues
Summer season begins again
An annual renewal of life
A history held within the lake

Remember those who lost their lives
They're never far away
The flow of life brought them close
Their memories here to stay

THE CLARITY OF THE LAKE

Yesterday, Sherry and I enjoyed a beautiful evening kayaking on Lake Carmi. Still water, blue skies, and the crisp air of early fall. Like our twisted times, the water here sometimes runs a bit murky. If I focus on the mire, it's all that I think about. Of course, those thoughts are unsettling because my desire for self-centered perfection does not align with the reality of the moment. The truth is, the water doesn't always run clear. Here at the lake and everywhere else.

It's easy to give in. To focus on the problems to look at the imperfections in a world full of chaos. To listen to the naysayers who fill the air with a vile and toxic spirit. Or, I can focus on the fullness of life and remember that it's up to me to determine my state of mind. Do I run down the rabbit hole of misery or opt to live within the spirit of hope?

In the flow of life there are choices to make. When anger rises, may it fuel justice, not harm. When sorrow comes, let it inspire growth, not self-pity. Every struggle is an opportunity. Live a life of kindness and love or one of hate and contempt? The choice is mine and the choice is yours.

If I allow myself the choice, the gift of life presents itself in profound beauty. The scenery of the moment is truly observed by the Grace of Divine Love. In silence it speaks in a clear voice. If I listen, direction on how to live and how best to experience life filter in.

The churn from a restless society fades away. The clarity of the lake shines with deep reflections of serenity. It plays a peaceful tune that settles into the soul. We live in a beautiful place that is full of Grace. May we allow ourselves to see it and be courageous enough to be it.

Take a Few Moments

Take a few moments
In the early morning
Slow down
Listen to the stories
Of the land
And the lake
They have much to say
In their silent voice
Whether on a mountaintop
On the misty water
Or here
In your own backyard
There is a way
That nature speaks
Whispers of Grace
It's not a magic
It doesn't sweep you away
It simply works its way
Into the one who is there
In the busy place

A drone of sadness
Unrest
Anxious chatter
In the fight to be right
Living in the present moment
Ordinary
Brilliant
Luminous
A poignant truthfulness
Comforting
Serene
Soothing
Tranquil
It's welcoming
This peaceful joy
Forget yourself
Become the quiet life
Bird song
Wing flaps
Ripples of rhythm
From the fish below
Waves of wisdom
Reverberate
Mysteriously
From holy men and women
No longer with us
Yet soulful mentors
All explanations fall away
Then, only love
We live in a beautiful place

Tell me about a time nature spoke to you...

A Pathway Through the Gate

This morning it's cold
Winter's chill is bright
Sunshine greets the day
Hoar frost reflects the light

Everywhere you look
Elegance leaves its mark
I wonder at the mystery
Of natures treasured ark

Little flicks of awe
From cosmic rays afar
Sprinkle through the scenery
Wondrous shooting stars

A pathway through a gate
In snows from yesterday
The tracks that we lay down
Merged by sagacious ways

Seeds of inspiration
Planted in our souls
Nurtured in the silence
Stories seldom told

Trace the path of blooming
Backwards through the night
The flowers of tomorrow
Today's bud holding tight

Stems of all the lessons
Connected to the roots
The way of all the knowledge
Kept beneath our boots

Footprints of the journey
A clear track set in snow
The wisdom of discovery
Held softly deep below

Once we start the journey
Investigation sparks
Choices from our pathways
Assembling the parts

The seeds of long ago
Germinate inside
Revealing reverent learning
The Spirit's gentle guide

Set about your course
As you make your way through life
If you follow thy will faithfully
Your road will have less strife

Release yourself from misery
From the gloomy toxic past
Embrace the subtle beauty
Joy is sure to last

Tranquility of presence
A visceral release
Serenity in moments
With Grace comes inner peace

AUTHOR BIO

Terry Lovelette was raised in Sheldon Springs, VT and currently lives in Saint Albans, VT. He loves the rolling hills of the Green Mountain State and holds them dear with a sense of loyalty. He is a graduate of Johnson State College. He is retired from a 44-year career in the semiconductor industry. He spent 21 years as a volunteer Assistant Coach for the University of Vermont's Men's Ice Hockey team. He also enjoyed volunteering his time as a USA Hockey Coaching Director in Vermont, as well as a volunteer coach for various youth sports teams. As a passionate outdoor enthusiast, he enjoys an interconnected relationship with nature. His passion has helped fuel a love for hiking. He has walked over 1,000 miles yearly in the last decade and a half.

Included in those journeys are through hikes of the Long Trail, The John Muir Trail, the Teton Crest Trail, and various other pathways in desert and mountainous areas of the US and Canada. He is the author of *Thoughts from a Walk – Green Mountain Musings* and *Down-Back*. His writings reflect the inspiration that comes from these journeys in a purposeful way.